Outreach and Identity: Evangelical Theological Monographs
World Evangelical Fellowship Theological Commission

Series Editor: Klaus Bockmuehl

No. 2 The Biblical Doctrine of Regeneration

The Biblical Doctrine of Regeneration

Helmut Burkhardt

Translated by O. R. Johnston

InterVarsity Press
Downers Grove, Illinois 60515
United States of America

The Paternoster Press
Exeter, England

CANADA: InterVarsity Press, 1875 Leslie Street,
Unit 10, Don Mills, Ontario M3B 2M5

AUSTRALIA: Emu Book Agencies, Pty., Ltd.,
63 Berry Street, Granville, 2142 N.S.W.

SOUTH AFRICA: Oxford University Press,
P.O. Box 1141, Cape Town

ISBN: 0-87784-322-8 (USA)

ISBN: 0-85364-235-4 (UK)

Made and printed in the United States of America
for InterVarsity Press, Downers Grove, IL 60515,
and for the Paternoster Press, Ltd., Paternoster House,
3 Mount Radford Crescent, Exeter, Devon, by The
Strathmore Company, 2000 Gary Lane, Geneva, IL 60134.

1

Regeneration— in Historical Perspective

"If one doctrine of our Christian faith is essential, then it is certainly that of regeneration. This is the spring from which everything which is good in our life must flow forth."[1] Philip Jacob Spener, father of pietism, made this statement as he began a long series of scriptural expositions on the topic of regeneration nearly three hundred years ago. Spener's pronouncement, however, has lost nothing of its urgency. It is a sentence which even today may well make the heart of a Christian beat faster.

Regeneration—a Word No Longer Heard?
In the course of time much of the theory and practice of pietism, from Bible studies to the topic of evangelization (much discussed in ecumenical circles), has obviously been absorbed by the life of the national church. The testimony to regeneration, however, has remained alien to all these discussions.

One has only to think of church publications. These tell us

much of the church and the world. Many a good biblical comment is expressed over many an important article of faith, often in a helpful, not merely superficial or critically destructive way. But I have yet to encounter the key word *regeneration* in this context.

This reticence concerning the testimony to regeneration also reaches into the circles of today's missionary-minded and well-taught Christians, and that seems to be especially significant. For example, the working party for national mission in the German Evangelical Church (EKD) has produced a pamphlet which outlines the principles and objectives of its work.[2] Here the task of proclamation of the gospel is described clearly and without compromise as "conversion" and "belief in Jesus Christ as Lord and Savior." And yet, even in the document about the spreading of the gospel[3] one thing is missing: the message of regeneration. How is this strange situation to be explained?

Regeneration—an Antiquated Word?
Is regeneration an antiquated word which fails to fit into the vocabulary of our technically minded world and which must be paraphrased in order to be understood? Does this explain the church's silence regarding regeneration?

Perhaps, but I doubt it. We do, in fact, meet in the modern world many things which remind us of the word *regeneration*. There is first the pervasive question of renewal in a general sense. People feel that we cannot go on living as we are today. Many are seeking paths to a new world. They expect thoroughgoing renewal through the alteration of relationships and structures, either through technical revolution or social revolution. The hope is that alteration of power and property relationships in favor of the workers will make society automatically more human. "The strengthened unification of the human species, more closely distributed over the planet, foreshadows not merely 'more of the same,' greater density, closer ties, etc. Rather, this growing unity is building up a pressure which is leading to the emergence of something genuinely new, which is neither predictable nor controllable. Only in retrospect can we say that at a certain point the quantitative developments crossed the line of qualitative changes . . . . Somewhere during the first half of the twentieth century the human species became a planetary entity and crossed over the irreversible line of no return, at which it gained its consciousness of being a species." Thus American theologian Philip Hefner describes the vision of the French biologist and philosopher Teilhard de Chardin.[4]

While here only changes in general human consciousness are being noted, in recent years reflections have also emerged about how one might change the very biological foundations of the human species. "The new eugenics allows us to consider the possibility of directing and accelerating the evolution of man. Eugenics is linked with the vision that 'in the future better generations of man will be created by man.' "[5]

These proposals for the future of humanity may be only dreams which will never be realized.[6] Yet they are to be taken seriously as the expression of a deep longing and seeking in our time. However, quite apart from the question whether such renewals are practicable, we are certainly entitled to ask, Are these developments desirable? Are these dreams in fact nightmares?

Do they not all bear a remarkably inhuman stamp? Not the individual, but humanity as a species is important. Humanity and the individual human character in it become the object of planning, of technology. A person becomes a "thing" out of which something must be "made."

The question of renewal, of human nature becoming different, is a burning issue of our time, leading up to formulas which immediately remind us of regeneration. And yet this seeking remains without direction and without hope.

The church, which surely has a word for a time such as this, is silent. Why?

Regeneration—an Arrogant Word?

Certainly there are many reasons why the church no longer talks about regeneration. These range from plain unbelief on the one hand to fear of what someone might think or say on the other.

One reason for this silence in the church, especially important and pervasive in churches of the reformed tradition, is a deep-rooted fear of Pharisaism. It is feared that whoever says anything about regeneration is making a distinction between two classes of people in the church: the regenerate and the unregenerate. The former must necessarily be considered somewhat better, more "Christian," than the latter. Moreover, the regenerate, according to this opinion, possess a certainty that repentance for specific sins is superfluous.

This fear has its justifiable origin in the central insight of the Reformation, that one can be counted righteous before God by faith alone and by nothing else. But as soon as any insight, however central, becomes generalized and made into a principle, a general law of thought, or a basic structural factor in a world view which must be applied everywhere and to everything, then there arises a sinister falsification of that originally correct and important insight. Starting from this one insight, a whole system has been built up, and all other insights are required to fit this system. The doctrine of regeneration in the course of the more recent history of theology seems to have become the victim of such a deviation. We see various forms of this deviation right up to our own time.

Reformation Theology

In the early stages of the Reformation, regeneration could be spoken of without embarrassment. In 1531 Luther wrote in his great exposition of the letter to the Galatians (on verse 4:7), "therefore . . . faith alone makes men sons of God, born of the Word."[7] And on Galatians 2:4: "If our opponents (that is, representatives of righteousness by works) will let us keep intact this faith by which we are born again, justified, and incorporated into Christ, we are willing to do anything. . . ."[8]

Regeneration is here seen to be part and parcel of the origin of faith through the word of the gospel proclamation which has been heard. The same idea can be found in many other similar passages in Luther. Thus, he seems to think of regeneration as an event in the life of adult persons. Actually, however, Luther's statements about regeneration are always fundamentally rooted in his understanding of baptism, and that implies the then regular practice of infant baptism. He says in "A Treatise on Baptism" in 1519, "The significance of baptism is a blessed dying unto sin and a resurrection in the grace of God, so that the old man, which is conceived and born in sin, is there drowned, and a new man, born in grace, comes forth and rises." At this point Luther refers to Titus 3 and John 3.[9] In this matter he stands squarely in the tradition of the early church and the middle ages, according to which baptism and regeneration are likewise intimately joined together.[10]

The connection between regeneration as an experience of a Christian sometimes long after baptism and its link with the past event of baptism, is to be found in Luther's dynamic understanding of this sacrament. Baptism *itself* stands at the beginning of the *work* of the sacrament,[11] which stretches over the whole life of the believer. A Christian's life is a continual new birth.[12] This understanding of regeneration as a dynamic process is made possible by Luther's view of human life as one single preparation for the life to come, which God inaugurates at the last day. Human life is a compressed moment when considered in the light of eternity.[13]

What was intended—in consequence of the Reformation's basic recognition of the radical lost condition of humanity—was a rejection of the medieval cast of mind which thought in terms of "substance,"[14] a rejection of the idea that a person in himself or herself counted for anything before God. This rejection was the very thing that was feared in pre-Reformation scholastic theology which spoke of an "indelible character" in the regenerate Christian.[15]

Surely it could be questioned whether what happened at the time of the Reformation in this respect was just a move from dependence on one philosophical tradition, that of the medieval metaphysic of being, into dependence on another, the radical historicalness of the ancient Greek philosopher Heraclitus, according to whom everything was only becoming and there was no abiding essence.[16] However that may be, one way or another this conception of regeneration as a dynamic process made it possible for the Reformation to speak from the very first about regeneration as something which not only stood at the beginning of life but was also decisively *being* effected in the Christian's life.

We also meet the word *regeneration* in the same sense in the confessional writings of the Reformation churches. For example, it constantly stands near central concepts like faith, conversion and justification.[17] And the Formula of Concord, that most significant second-generation Reformation work, in which the reformational confession-making of Lutheran stamp found its mature completion, expressly defends the work of regeneration against the misunderstanding that it is the work of man[18] and distinguishes clearly between the regenerate and the unregenerate.[19]

In the long run, however, the great tension in which the

Reformation understanding of regeneration stood could not be continued. ,An additional complication came when enthusiastic groups appealed one-sidedly to regeneration as an experience independent of the external means of salvation of word and sacrament. In conflict with them, ecclesiastical theology came increasingly to restrict regeneration to baptism. Since adult baptism scarcely occurred in practice, that meant infant baptism. In order to defend the "by grace alone" formula from the danger of the enthusiasts, regeneration was torn from the reach and the experience of the individual.

The doctrine of baptismal regeneration took over the leading position in the church's doctrine and became the accepted orthodoxy. Since then, consciously or unconsciously, it has been the most important foundation of popular piety.[20]

Liberal Theology

Regeneration apparently was understood quite differently in the liberal theology of the latter part of the nineteenth century. In his *Instruction in the Christian Religion* the man who was probably the most significant representative of this theology, Albrecht Ritschl, wrote, "What individuals regard as the beginning is at the best to be considered only as a step in their Christian development."[21]

This places regeneration squarely within the life of the individual Christian. But already in the concept of "development" there lies a tendency to level down regeneration into what finally becomes an uninterrupted series of linked experiences. Regeneration is the result of Christian education and cannot be pinpointed within an individual's experience.

The reason for this sounds very much like a Reformation statement: "It is necessary to be on one's guard against wishing to make certain of this foundation of one's own Christian life by direct experience or at a definite time. . . . Thus for the one who attains to independence of his Christian life through the innumerable means of education belonging to the Christian community, it is quite impossible as well as unnecessary to mark the beginning of this result."[22] But the note "all of grace" is here generalized and set in the framework of the idealistic philosophy of Ritschl's time, and hence the biblical teaching on regeneration has the sting of offense taken from it.

In the general popular consciousness this inclusion of regeneration within the framework of evolutionary thought has caused it to take on the following form: At bottom it is presumption to say, "I am a Christian." At best we may say only that we are on the way to becoming such. So, according to this view, people are not divided into Christians and non-Christians but rather into better and worse Christians, and (given the danger of Pharisaism) the latter is the better.

Dialectical Theology

When after the First World War the predominance of liberal theology was superseded by dialectical theology, the orthodox teaching of regeneration lived on in another new form. Instead of regeneration being placed within an event in the past (infant baptism), it was now transferred to the realm of the ever-resounding divine word of promise. It became commonplace to say, "Regeneration is not conceivable. It lies beyond human understanding and experience."

Thus Karl Barth, in an exposition of the Confession of Faith on the question, In what does the continuity in the life of the regenerate-yet-also-natural man consist? says, "Fundamentally it might . . . be said with regard to the continuity between the two that God's having *patience* with me is the basis of it, God's letting me still have time to make this turn."[23] "Each day anew in every fresh situation the sinful man in his totality will stand face to face with the grace of

Christ in its totality."[24]

Barth's pupil and friend, Otto Weber, citing as evidence John 3:8, writes in his *Dogmatics,* "The regenerate as such cannot be grasped."[25] Regeneration "belongs to the reality which is present with us only as the reality we await."[26] "Nothing here is conceivable. But it is all 'within sight.' "[27] Here, even more strongly than in the writings of Barth, the supernatural quality of regeneration becomes entirely future. It is only another short step to the position of Weber's pupil Jürgen Moltmann and his "theology of hope." In that theology we do not meet the key word *regeneration*—not at any rate in that particular book. It is significant, however, to note that the goal of missionary proclamation is circumscribed "so that no corner of this world should remain without God's promise of new creation through the power of the resurrection."[28]

Regeneration is either left out or conceived of as an event, or more exactly the hope of an event, of future renewal which comprehends the whole world. The salvation which it brings, however, "does not mean merely salvation of the soul, individual rescue from this evil world, comfort for the troubled conscience, but also the realization of the eschatological hope of justice, the humanizing of man, the socializing of humanity, peace for all creation."[29]

In spite of the balance provided by the "not only . . . but also" construction, Moltmann's deeper interest clearly lies with the second half of the sentence. The first half merely presents a row of partly sneering clichés. The fear of Pharisaism here takes on another shape: that of the fear of self-centeredness in salvation and self-sufficiency. Yet it has the same effect—the witness to regeneration has no proper place here. When the word *regeneration* arises, must thoughts of self-centered salvation, arrogance and Pharisaism necessarily arise also? Is it really a presumptuous word? In the following section the simple attempt will be made to question Holy Scripture on this matter to find out what is understood there on the subject of regeneration. This alone can be normative for what Christianity says about it.

2

Regeneration— the Biblical Testimony

Regeneration—a Biblical Concept?

A quick glance at a concordance yields an astoundingly meager result: in the whole of the Old Testament the word *regeneration* does not appear at all, and in the New Testament it occurs only twice. Moreover, each of these two passages is to be understood in a sense completely different from the other.

The first occurs in St. Matthew's Gospel in the story of the rich young ruler. In the subsequent conversation between Jesus and his disciples, Peter says, "We have left everything and followed You; what then will there be for us?" Jesus answers, "Truly I say to you, that you who have followed Me, in the *regeneration* when the Son of Man will sit on His glorious throne, you also shall sit upon twelve thrones, judging the twelve tribes of Israel" (Mt. 19:27-28). Regeneration here is equated with the renewal of the whole creation which is linked with the last judgment at the end of time.[30]

The other passage is Titus 3:5, where the apostle speaks

of the "washing of regeneration." In contrast to its significance in Matthew 19:28, regeneration here is a present dimension—a dimension which refers back to an event in the past ("saved us").

With only two occurrences of the word in Scripture, is the concept of regeneration only a phenomenon on the outer edge of Scripture, and therefore quite rightly relegated to a similar position in the life of the church? The objections of many expositors of the New Testament could point us in the same direction. They note that the idea of rebirth was a common one in the world of oriental Greek religions, into which youthful Christianity burst. However, the literary and archeological proofs are less numerous than this theory would lead us to expect.[31]

Another observation is more important: the word *regeneration* is not by any means as lonely and unsupported in Scripture as the first findings in a dictionary search might lead us to expect. The biblical context makes the word quite distinct from possible occurrences in other religions and clarifies its important function within the total biblical testimony.

Two passages in 1 Peter come closest to expressing the concept of regeneration. Although the noun *regeneration* is not used, a corresponding verb is: "Blessed be the God and Father of our Lord Jesus Christ, who according to His great mercy *has caused us to be born again* to a living hope through the resurrection of Jesus Christ from the dead" (1 Pet. 1:3). Peter writes, further, that "you *have been born again* not of seed which is perishable but imperishable, that is, through the living and abiding word of God" (1:23). In both passages the Greek word *anagennan* is used ("to beget again or anew"). In this word the thought of rebirth is even more clearly expressed than in the Greek noun *palingenesia* which literally points to a re-origination but then came to be used in the sense of rebirth or begetting again.[32]

In a similar fashion, James writes of a begetting through the word: "In the exercise of His will He brought us forth by the word of truth" (Jas. 1:18).

Further evidence is found in probably the best-known biblical passage testifying to regeneration, John 3:3-7. Mention is made of being born "again" or "from above" or "anew." In addition there are many passages in the writings of John which simply speak of "being born" of God (Jn. 1:13; 3:5, 6, 8; 1 Jn. 2:29; 3:9; 4:7; 5:1, 4, 18).

Some biblical passages are concerned in the same breath, as a kind of explanatory parallel, both with *becoming* and with *being* a child of God. This connection seems to me to be very important. (See Jn. 1:12; 1 Jn. 3:1-2 [cf. 2:29]; 3:10 [cf. v. 9]; 5:2 [cf. vv. 1 and 4]). And so the area contained by the word *regeneration* has been considerably enlarged.

Finally, in connection with the testimony of John to the experience of being rebegotten by God and being a child of God, we must include the great letters of Paul and above all Galatians 3:26—4:7 and Romans 8:14-17, 29.

What Is Regeneration?

In order to work out the significance of the biblical testimony to regeneration, we shall in the following section select some of the passages just referred to, ask what they offer for our understanding of regeneration and expound this briefly.

Titus 3:3-7. A cursory glance at Titus 3 already has shown us that rebirth is an event lying in the past ("he saved us . . . by the washing of regeneration," v. 5). Moreover, this is an event in the past for those who belong to the church. (For according to the context, Paul and Titus, as well as those entrusted to the care of the latter, are members of the fellowship.)

This event marked a sharp break in the life of the individual. The time after this event ("But when . . . appeared," v. 4) is contrasted with the time before this event ("We also once were . . . " v. 3). The latter condition is characterized by a catalog of vices: "We also once were foolish ourselves, disobedient, deceived, enslaved to various lusts and pleasures, spending our life in malice and envy, hateful, hating one another" (v. 3).

Regeneration has come into this life as a great disruption, working itself out in the realm of the visible and the empirical. Those characteristics just enumerated are no longer appropriate for the Christian's life after this break; they stand under the word "once." The "now" on the contrary is characterized by the qualities indicated in Titus 2:1-6: "sound in faith, in love, in perseverance" (see also 1 Pet. 2:1-2).

This change, however, has not come about by a person deciding to do this and to abandon the other. Expressly and unambiguously the apostle says in 3:5, "not on the basis of deeds which we have done in righteousness." Therefore, it is not expected that we should in the first place make ourselves better. There is not the slightest suggestion of any preliminary condition on our part. Only one simple and plainly basic preliminary condition is mentioned: the historic appearance of Jesus Christ our Savior (v. 6), the "incarnate goodness of God"[33] as we might call it. The change in people's lives is exclusively caused by this invasion of God.

This viewpoint is underlined by the fact that the little catalog of virtues (goodness, kindness, mercy) which follows the catalog of vices in verse 3 characterizes in the first place nothing but the disposition of God. Everything begins with *God* being like that.

The explanation of what comprises this saving invasion is given by two parallel clauses in verse 5: "washing of regeneration" and "renewing by the Holy Spirit." The genitive in the second clause denotes the active subject: it is the Holy Spirit who is here at work renewing people. This renewal is therefore paraphrased in the first clause by a picture or, more precisely, in two pictures, the image of *washing* leading to the image of *rebirth*.

According to the conviction of most expositors, the image of washing or bathing means that baptism is in view here. This recognition should not be contested on behalf of any particular position in the controversy about infant baptism and baptismal regeneration. For this question cannot in any way be decided from the simple recognition of the close connection between baptism and regeneration found in this passage. That there was a close connection between baptism and the Holy Spirit in one way or another in primitive Christianity is more or less taken for granted and is especially evident in the Acts of the Apostles.[34] But this cannot decide the question whether the same is therefore valid today in a completely different situation within the church.

One thing can be learned from the connection between baptism and regeneration as witnessed to by the Christian congregation at that time: baptism points back to the beginning of the Christian condition, to a once and for all, unrepeatable beginning.

At the same time, baptism makes the connection between the statements about regeneration and another important biblical tradition—the idea of dying (and rising again) with Christ—found in Romans 6 and Colossians 3. The origin of new life in regeneration therefore has to do with dying to an old way of life.

Finally, verse 7 gives the goal of regeneration: "that . . . we might be made heirs according to the hope of eternal life." Eternal life is not simply endless life. In addition to this merely temporal concept, it suggests a much fuller and richer idea: life in undisturbed fellowship with God. In regeneration we could say that the legal basis ("heir" is a legal concept) has been laid for our participation in this life. Thus we are taken out of the thinking, hoping and fearing which centers solely upon ourselves and our world, and are taken into the plans and purposes of God.

In this connection, one precondition[35] is mentioned here which is related to the individual and clearly regarded as given in regeneration: "justified by His [Jesus'] grace" (v. 7). Through this word *justified* a connection again is made with another important biblical tradition concerning the way of salvation: in regeneration the justification of the sinner by grace alone is being consummated.

This context widens once more the horizon within which we have to understand regeneration. In regeneration something happens which is directed toward the day of God's final judgment over the whole world. Already, therefore, a relationship has been established with the Judge of all the world; "justified" denotes a new personal relationship between man and God. The threatening question of guilt has now been clarified. A treaty has been made, as it were, a covenant entered into, which is founded securely and purely upon grace.

In sum, then, three principles can be derived from this discussion. First, regeneration is a temporal and once and for all change in the life of the individual. It is a new beginning which results in visible changes in moral behavior. Second, this change has its roots in the unilateral initiative of the triune God.[36] Third, the reborn person, now justified, stands in a new relationship to God. Rebirth is a personal category, not a natural or magical category.

In regeneration, then, we are not dealing with a renewal of persons in themselves or with change itself. Nor first and foremost are we dealing with personal development or liberation from self-alienation. First and foremost we are dealing with the ending of an alienation from God and centrally with the complete renewal of relationship with God.

John 3:1-16. Verse 3 of this passage lays down with pointed brevity that by nature we cannot "see" the kingdom of God, that is, we cannot get into it (v. 5b; see also Jn. 3:36; Lk. 2:26; Acts 2:27; 1 Pet. 3:10).

Verse 6 explains this present human condition as *sarx* ("flesh"). By this word, people are designated from one aspect as creatures characterized by impermanence and transience (see 1 Pet. 1:24). At the same time, however, they are designated here as creatures who rebel against their Creator, and find themselves in the situation of the people of Israel grumbling in the wilderness (v. 14), having therefore already come under judgment (v. 18b).

This ruin in sin is so complete, that only new[37] birth,[38] a total root-and-branch renewal of the whole person (vv. 3-8) can bring salvation. The mention of water in verse 5 is another hint at baptism (see Jn. 4:1) and thereby at the dying of the "old man" in repentance.[39] Right up to our own day this has been an extremely offensive statement: all our practical energy and enthusiasm for renewal and reform is doomed to founder in God's eyes. No increase of our strength can really help us further. We must first die to our own efforts and our own hopes.

However, the new birth is now positively announced as the decisive change of direction brought about by the work of the Spirit of God (vv. 5-6, 8). Being effected by the Spirit, it remains secret in its origin: "The wind blows where it wishes and you hear the sound of it, but do not know where it comes from and where it is going" (v. 8a). It is a miracle, radically removed beyond our power to bring it about, just as the complete ruin due to sin and the way in which the Spirit of God works in secret are beyond our control.

Yet Jesus does not stop at the negative answer to the question, "How?" asked by Nicodemus. "We speak that which we know," he says, "and bear witness of that which we have seen" (v. 11). In verses 15 and 16 follows the hint at the lifting up of the Son of man and the invitation to faith in the Son of God who is given for us.

At this point any remaining confusion due to purely formal or technical misunderstanding of rebirth is blasted away. Regeneration is accomplished wherever a person comes to faith in Jesus, who has borne the sins of the world and, therefore, mine also, on the cross (Jn. 1:29).

> And now things stand just as in the story of the serpent in the wilderness: those who had been bitten by the serpents looked up to the brazen serpent and stayed alive. To gaze on the crucified and risen Son of Man means eternal life. He has taken all claims and power from the powers of death which cast their spell over us. We see him—he is pictured before our very eyes—as often as we hear his Word. It is his will to be present there in person; and one can believe in him and trust him as a present Saviour.[40]

In just the same way the key words in verse 16, *love* from God's side and *faith* from man's side, refer to an extremely personal happening.

This is not an explanation of the miracle of regeneration. The love of God for sinners is indeed unfathomable, miraculous in the truest sense of the word. But a double misunderstanding of this miracle must be rejected. The "transcendentalistic" misunderstanding says that regeneration is and remains a purely supernatural, unexperienced and unrecognizable event. The context shows that this popular understanding of John 3:8 is not tenable. On the other side is the magical misunderstanding, in which it is believed that if only some specific, appointed thing is done—whether water baptism or repetition of a prayer of dedication—the miracle will take place automatically, so to speak.

Regeneration is an essentially personal happening between God and the individual. Being an event of this nature, it is tied to the Word (vv. 11-13; see also 1 Pet. 1:23-24; Jas. 1:18). Yet at the same time, it is also in a certain sense always "reasonable" too, inasmuch as words aim at understanding.

Strangely, the conversation of Jesus with Nicodemus breaks off without any further consideration being given to the success of its impact on Nicodemus himself.[41] Perhaps, however, the narrative of the Samaritan woman in John 4 may serve as an example of how the principles expounded in John 3 are accomplished in the life of an individual awakening to a consciousness of guilt and to the revealing of the Savior of the world (4:18, 42).

Galatians 4:1-7. Contrary to the suppositions of many expositors,[42] Paul too knows how to speak of birth from God. According to Galatians 4:29, the one born of the flesh persecuted "him who was born according to the Spirit."[43] And those who came to faith through Paul he calls his children whom the Holy Spirit, through Paul's testimony, has "begotten" (1 Cor. 4:15; Gal. 4:19; Philem. 10). Just as in 1 John the children of God and the children of the devil are contrasted (3:10), so Paul sets the children of light over against the children of a "crooked and perverse generation" (Phil. 2:15; cf. 1 Thess. 5:5).

In addition, however, we meet a quite different contrast: that between child and slave (Gal. 4:7). The viewpoint here is different from John's. Paul is concerned not with the origin of the sonship (*ed theou,* that is, "from God,"), but with the believers' present position. And in contradistinction to the status of the slave, their position is characterized as that of free persons. They are free from the law as a means of salvation and free from the necessity of enforced obedience to God through law and the threat of judgment (cf. Gal. 4:21ff.; 5:1).

Similarly, Paul speaks in Romans 8 of the glorious liberty of the children of God (v. 21). The prayer "Abba! Father!"

(Rom. 8:15; Gal. 4:6) is rooted in the certainty of God's love and is an expression of this new, inner free relationship to God. At the same time, however, it is an expression of obligation which goes well beyond merely legal concepts like justification and inheritance.

Yet from Paul's slave/child contrast this much is clear: for him the concept "child" implies no prior act of begetting. "Child" is rather a pictorial description of a present condition, and *huiothesia* (Gal. 4:5) can also have the significance of a legal status resulting from adoption ("adoption as sons").[44] Since regeneration is described by means of the image of adoption as well as the act of begetting a child, it becomes clear that the biblical testimony to regeneration is pictorial in character, not literal.

The recognition of this keeps us from one possible unbalanced interpretation of the word regeneration. Taken literally in the full sense of the word, regeneration might be understood as a directly physical/biological event. The regenerate person would then be quite different in himself, of divine quality and substance.[45] The difference between creator and creature would be removed, the sin which is still active even in Christians (Rom. 7) would be represented as innocuous, and people would be enticed into independence[46] and arrogant self-sufficient security before God. Apostasy, a possibility with which the New Testament obviously reckons, would have become impossible or only thinkable as a miracle of reverse transformation. But there is no trace of such a meaning for apostasy in Scripture.

We are kept from all these false tracks if we hold in mind this one thing: regeneration is no independent event alongside others, such as calling, justification or sanctification. These latter concepts are to be understood in a stricter sense than is regeneration. *But, regeneration is* a vivid image for something which can be designated together with other concepts and must be held in close connection with them and understood with them.

What Is Irreplaceable in the Image "Regeneration"?

After what has been said above, the impression may first arise that the understanding of the testimony to regeneration should be dissolved into a mere change of relationship, the regenerated person remaining essentially the same.

But what is the essence of this person really? The conjecture that regeneration is a mere change of relationship presupposes one definite, widely accepted answer to this question: a person is a complete, indivisible essence (*individuum*), who in the last analysis is a creative independent absolute Ego. This view of humanity lies at the root of the misunderstandings of regeneration sketched above and plays a fateful role in them.

In fact, this description of a person contradicts the picture which is drawn in the Bible. According to the Bible, a person is a dependent being in every respect, standing in manifold and indissoluble relationships in every part of his or her existence. First and foremost what distinguishes a human being from other creatures—non-negotiable existence as an individual person—does not consist in any necessary way in being an independent self. Rather, this uniqueness consists in being set in relationship to a significant Other, that is, to fellow humans and above all to God.

So then, we have explained regeneration as the start of a new relationship with God. And this new relationship is to be seen against the background of the open concept of a person which we have sketched out above. It is not something which a person puts on, so to speak, like a coat (as if a totally independent being were to add a relationship to someone), but something which determines and changes those relationships which constitute his or her innermost being.

But now, back to the question raised at the outset of this section: are regeneration (on the one side) and justification and sanctification (on the other) interchangeable concepts, so that one could drop the first (and, possibly, more problematic) concept? Or is there something irreplaceable in the image of regeneration?

We answer, first, that in no other image entering this discussion is the *unilateral activity* of God in salvation and the passivity of the individual so clearly expressed. While Scripture does challenge us to be converted,[47] we never meet the word *regeneration* or a corresponding verb in an imperative form. Regeneration, therefore, denotes the saving and renewal of persons as the sole work of God through Jesus Christ in the Holy Spirit.

Second, no other image expresses so emphatically the *newness* of the Christian's life as that of new birth. Elsewhere the statements about the "new creation" (Gal. 6:15; 2 Cor. 5:17) probably come nearest.

Nor does any other word show so clearly how by nature we have incurred the liability to death and judgment. "Improvement" is no longer sufficient; any mere evolution or development is hopeless.

Occasionally it is retorted that painting such a black picture devalues the person and leads into a dangerous passivity. But this is only a tactical argument which avoids the reality of our condition and whitewashes our situation before God. This whitewashing is perhaps the most deeply damaging element in the present-day proclamation of the church. The message of regeneration sternly puts its finger upon this perilous wound.

Third, no verbal image designates so clearly the *historicalness of the new life*. It is occasionally said that regeneration is a process which comprehends the whole life of a human being (see above, pp. 11-16ff.). But this meaning flatly contradicts not only the meaning of the word itself (no one is being born continuously), but also, as we have seen, it is not justified by the scriptural context. Rather, regeneration is the unrepeatable, once and for all, historical beginning of the new life. That is, it is the beginning of both justification and sanctification.

Viewed in this light, even the occasional equivalence of regeneration with justification[48] or with sanctification[49] is not tenable. Both of these cover the whole life of the Christian, who is daily within the process of sanctification. In the same way, the Christian daily needs—and will need until the last moment of earthly life—the forgiveness of sins. Regeneration, however, stands at the beginning of this process and only there.

It is sometimes asked what form regeneration will take in the life of different individuals. According to the witness of the New Testament (perhaps also corresponding to the situation of the church at that time), regeneration is normally an event compressed into a short span of time, as indeed the connection with baptism shows. But in addition, the work of the Spirit in regeneration can continue over a longer time. Indeed, from the outside it can take on the appearance of a development. However, it is never a development of what is naturally present, but always takes a person through a fundamental break which sooner or later becomes clearly visible. If regeneration is understood as a single experiential event, there emerges the possibility of a distinction between the regenerate and the not-yet regenerate.

As a rule this conclusion meets with passionate contradiction within the church. We have seen that this contradiction has no basis in Scripture. Contrary arguments often presuppose a false understanding of regeneration, as if it were a human work. This contradiction frequently gains its emotional power from an inner repugnance of fallen human nature:

After all, there are very few people in our country who like a worldly pastor, one who lets everything pass and who dishes out a milky mixture containing neither thought nor seriousness. People like those pastors who speak sternly and appealingly, best of all perhaps when the tears trickle down the cheeks of both the speaker and the listeners.[50] Note well that this is the case only as long as the pastor speaks sternly and yet avoids mentioning conversion and the new birth, avoids making the biblical distinction between regenerate and unregenerate men.[51]

The church has to a great extent become an educational institution in which one can learn quite a number of things step by step and in which one is urged to do this or that. Let no one despise such procedures. The church fulfills a cultural function in this way, a function which lies squarely within the will of God as expressed in the First Article of the Apostles' Creed. But it is sinister if the decisive question concerning eternal salvation is passed over and thereby the doctrine of regeneration is laid aside.

Fourth, regeneration *inaugurates* the personal relationship between the individual Christian and God called sonship or the father/child relationship. This relationship is distinguished by several characteristics.

(a) The *factor of duration* is strongly present in the word regeneration.[52] Sonship is something lasting, something which cannot be canceled, in distinction, for example, from friendship. Sonship is a statement about being. Philosophically expressed, it is a directly ontological category (cf. especially 1 Jn. 3:1-2). Being a Christian by no means consists merely in a process of becoming but certainly in a state of being as well.

This is not in any way to suggest that the regenerate person is already perfect, without sin. The expression *simul justus et peccator* ("at once righteous and a sinner") is properly in fact a title which only fits the reborn. Only in the regenerate does that battle begin which is depicted so movingly in Romans 7. But he who one day will finally release us from this conflict, Jesus, has by the Holy Spirit even now really entered the life of the Christian.

The new life which has thereby arisen is concentrated in the first place in the personal realm, while the physical and cosmic dimension is even more strongly an object of hope: "It has not appeared as yet what we shall be" (1 Jn. 3:2; cf. also Rom. 8:23; Mt. 19:28). The Christian is not yet a perfect child of God, but is perfectly a child of God.[53]

(b) The relationship between the Christian and God is also expressed in the call which springs from the *freedom of the children of God*. "Abba! Father!" is a more adequate expression for the reality of the new life than all the abstractions of the doctrine of justification.

(c) The *social aspect* of this relationship is particularly noteworthy in our contemporary dialog. This aspect of the state of the children of God is rooted in the biblical testimony to regeneration and finds its classic expression in 1 John 5:1: "Whoever believes that Jesus is the Christ is born of God; and whoever loves the Father loves the child born of Him" (see also 1 Pet. 1:22-23).

Though the Christian is first of all in view here, nevertheless the concept of being born into a family gives all people, Christian or not, a demonstration of an organic approach to the realization of human community free from self-interest. No other concept used to describe the attaining of salvation brings this social aspect into the discussion in quite the same way—neither the concept of justification nor that of sanctification.

The message of brotherhood based on common sonship of God is the expression of a most profound mutual obligation, for it exists within God himself. For this reason, however, it is also an expression of the most powerful unity and, therefore, is removed from the power of our own arbitrary disposal. Brotherhood cannot be renounced, unless it be through one or another falling from faith itself. Brotherhood can be made more difficult, it can be distorted, it can be buried, but it is not possible to dissolve it like a friendship. We do not decide about brotherhood. Another person has decided it for us—in our regeneration.

Though our abstracting modes of thought may tempt us to think that *regeneration* is a dispensable term, the testimony of the Bible itself shows that regeneration is irreplaceable by any other idea.

Regeneration in God's Plan of Salvation

We have examined the biblical teaching on regeneration in some detail. We now need to step back a little in order to get a view of its ranking in the overall testimony of Scripture.

We have already seen that the testimony to regeneration does not occur in the Old Testament. That is no mere chance. In the Old Testament from the election of Abraham ("I will make you a great nation," Gen. 12:2) the people as a whole is in the first place the object of God's election and salvation. And, of course, there is talk of an outpouring of the Spirit (Joel 3; Is. 44; Ezek. 36), of renewal, and even the renewal of the heart (Jer. 31). This is especially evident in the message of the great prophets about God's future activity.

At this stage of God's revelation, Scripture nowhere speaks of the Spirit's work in this respect as a present reality, but rather as promise for the future. Moreover, it is Israel as a whole that is always primarily in view and not so much the individual within Israel.

Much nearer to the New Testament testimony to regeneration is Psalm 51:10: "Create in me a clean heart, O God, and renew a steadfast spirit within me." But despite the formal proximity, what is spoken of here is not regeneration in the full sense.[54]

The most likely genuine exception seems to be Psalm 2:7: "Thou art My Son, today have I begotten Thee." But this passage refers not to any individual in Israel, but exclusively to the anointed one of God and, in prophetic understanding of this testimony, to the Messiah who was to appear at the end of time and, finally, to the only Son (Heb. 1:5).

Granted, we do occasionally find in the Old Testament the ideal of "children [that is, sons] of God" (Deut. 14:1; Hos. 1:10). But even this expression refers each time to the whole nation of Israel and serves as an expression of its election (cf. Deut. 14:2; 32:5-6).

Of what significance, then, to the whole witness of Scripture is the appearance of the testimony to regeneration in the New Testament? By ascertaining that the word *regeneration* is only a New Testament word, I do not mean to devalue the Old Testament or to contest its character as revelation in any way. To observe a difference between the Old and New Testaments at this point does not in any way imply a theological evaluation. It simply points to the historicalness of the Bible. The Bible is not a systematic textbook of doctrine, but tells the story of the ways of God for our salvation. The specific difference is due to this: that God at one time took a different way from that which he adopted at another time.

The whole Old Testament is, above all, stamped with the mark of one particular way: that of God's choosing the people of Israel. This way began with the call of the father of the people, Abraham, and ended at least for the present time (cf. Rom. 11) in front of the gates of Jerusalem when Jesus uttered his woes over this city (Mt. 23:37ff.).

The new way of God was at the same time prepared. Its decisive and abiding precondition was the sending of the Son and his suffering and death for the sins of his people and of the whole world. The realization of this new way is indicated with special emphasis through the key word *regeneration*. But in what does the novelty of this way consist, compared with the previous way? We may answer this question in three parts.

1. Individualization. The key word *regeneration* indicates that there is an individualization about the means God is using. His method with the people as a whole had foundered on the repeated revolt of the people. Therefore God switched over to guerilla tactics, so to speak, conquering person by person. God fights for the individual in order to make the individual the tool of his saving will for the whole of humanity.

Today we are discovering again that humans are community beings and the collectives and cooperatives are accepted notions. In many respects this is a good development. Individualization in regeneration, indeed, is not the final goal of God's ways but a part of the way. To be sure, according to the biblical testimony it is an essential part of the way. One might object that, since the New Testament, this way of the individual could not be understood quite independently of God's decrees. It could as well be seen as the result of a long history of intellectual development with many foreshadowings. In the thinking of Israel, for example, one can discover individualizing tendencies,[55] since the so-called Solomonic enlightenment[56] and above all in the wisdom literature.[57] During the exile, also, when for the exiles the Holy Land and the central Holy Place in Jerusalem had been lost, there arose instead a concentration of piety on the individual's obedience to the law.[58] This pious devotion to the law later (under Hellenistic influence?) joined with the wisdom tradition. In this tradition anyone righteous through God-fearing deeds could be designated a child of God (see Wisdom 2:13).

But the decree of God and the (suggested) historical development need not be mutually exclusive possibilities. This historical development itself may be a decree of God. On the other hand, Scripture indicates that God accommodates himself to the ways of his people, even their mistaken ways, as, for example, when Israel demanded a king "like all the nations" and God gave them one (1 Sam. 8:5, 19ff.).

This individualization, therefore, need not in any sense be understood as a development toward some higher form of religious insight. For God, at any rate, it is first and foremost the very opposite. Self-limitation, self-restriction, even self-abasement turn out to be the way of the Creator of the world in choosing his people. These same characteristics are all the more true and appropriate in his way with the individual. The suffering of God over his people (Is. 43:24ff.) now multiplies itself countless times.

An individualization of God's way does not by any means signify that Christians wander around in the world as scattered individuals, making the church at best simply the sum total of such individuals.[59] In fact, New Testament exegesis in recent decades has recognized that the church is not merely the sum of her members, but has priority before the individual.[60] Even the Old Testament idea of the people of God can be applied to the church.[61] But this does not happen in the same sense as in the Old Testament. However true it may be that the boundaries of the church in the New Testament cannot be clearly drawn in detail, the actual belonging to her in principle is inseparable from faith and therefore from regeneration.

2. Radicalization. Furthermore, *regeneration* indicates a radicalization of one's relationship to God. The basis for the relationship to God which is given in regeneration is not only the uncaused, electing love of God found also under the old covenant (where it is shown especially toward the insignificant and the poor[62]). Beyond this, God's radical, uncon-

ditional love reaches its height in the love of God even for his enemies (Rom. 5:10). Indeed, God's self-binding love for his enemies goes beyond even the wisdom saying of Jesus in Matthew 5:45: "For He causes His sun to rise on the evil and the good." This again has its historic basis and confirmation in the atoning sacrifice of the Son on the cross.

The incomparable freedom of the children of God, and therefore the real novelty of the life which is given to us in regeneration, is rooted in this certainty concerning God's love for his enemies. Our relationship to God is at this point not based on any prior or later achievement but on grace, and therefore on faith alone.

In such a commitment to the individual given in regeneration God risks much, namely, a lasting exposure to ridicule. And yet he gains much more at the same time—the free love of his children.

3. Regeneration and God's universal purpose. In pointing out the individual aspect of regeneration the universal purpose of God is in no way forgotten. On the contrary, this understanding of the seriousness of the human predicament keeps in sight the only realistic way to God. In a certain way the universal purpose is even further underscored by the individualization: while God calls individuals of all nations to become his children independently of their origin, at the same time he calls them everywhere into his service as witnesses of his coming world-embracing rule and as cells of continuing renewal. "So that we [with a view to the final new creation] might be, as it were, the first fruits among His creatures" (Jas. 1:18).

This perspective provides justification for the social involvement of the Christian. Regeneration places the Christian within the broad horizon of the saving will of God for humanity and creation. But this individual or particular approach may not be overhastily and enthusiastically omitted through an attempt to be long-sighted or to attain a "broad vision."[63] God's universal renewing work goes through the needle's eye of a genuine renewal of the individual in regeneration.

How Can the Regenerate Be Recognized?

So far I have tried to unfold the biblical teaching on regeneration in its depth and breadth. I should like once more to bring matters to a head somewhat contentiously by selecting the two points which seem to me to be in special need of recall and which need to be cleared of any tendentious distortion:

First, regeneration is a *real* change in the life of a person. It is not merely intended[64] change, nor is it only asserted[65] or expected[66] change (see above, p. 15, Otto Weber).

Second, regeneration is a *once and for all* event at the beginning of the Christian life and not a development or a lifelong process.

Granted, regeneration is not so readily accessible to our recognition and consciousness as is conversion.[67] Since conversion and regeneration cannot in my view be separated from each other timewise, regeneration might be called the hidden side of conversion.[68] Nevertheless, as a real, once and for all event, it is not fundamentally or in principle hidden from our recognition. Accordingly, a distinction between the regenerate and the unregenerate is possible in principle.

The reservations which usually arise against this distinction have already been mentioned. It is feared that one would of necessity drop into a spirit of judgment and Pharisaism. Normally, however, the reality seems to be the other way around: the seemingly pious hesitance to recognize the regenerate/unregenerate distinction despises and denies the work and the way of God in us and with us.

On the other hand, it is obvious that recognition of this distinction could lead to false judging. This danger becomes especially acute wherever that distinction hinges on outward expressions of the new life, particularly if it concerns questions of lifestyle, to which no answers can or need be found which are binding upon all Christians.

This concession does not mean that the way the Christian leads his or her life, even in its peripheral aspects, is being placed at his or her own discretion or whim. But a really clear picture of the regenerate person has not yet emerged. Changing a verse from the letter of James, "Even the heathen do good—and tremble" (see Jas. 2:19).

In order to avoid this confusion as well as the danger of wrongful judging we must probe more deeply, not by asking, *How* does the Christian live in detail? but, *On what* does he or she live, basically? In regeneration a fundamental decision has taken place in the life of the individual engaged in the battle between the flesh and the spirit, between love of self on the one hand and love of God and neighbor on the other.[69] The battle continues; indeed, it only now begins properly. But, in principle, matters are clear: the believer now lives in the law of the Spirit (Rom. 8:2), in the law of freedom (Jas. 1:25; 2:12). This freedom, however, means essentially having a will which is free to live before God.

This freedom of the will is circumscribed first by an independent longing of regenerate persons for the Word of God. Just as they have been begotten by the Word (cf. 1 Pet. 1:23; Jas. 1:18), so they recognize their ongoing dependence on the Word, on God addressing them.

The regenerate person's freedom of the will is further circumscribed by an independent longing for prayer.[70] Just as a child feels an urge to call on its father, so the regenerate feels an urge to call on God and to speak with him (Gal. 4:6; Rom. 8:15).

Finally, this freedom of will is circumscribed by an independent longing of the regenerate for fellowship with the other children of God (1 Jn. 5:1ff.; 1 Thess. 4:9).

Those who have been regenerated live in and from these three basic characteristics. Without them they are like fish lying on the sand.

Regeneration is neither an antiquated nor an arrogant nor a self-sufficient word. Rather, it is a word which, if read in its biblical context, leads us to the heart of the gospel, the message of God's salvation for this world. *Regeneration* is a word for which the church has really no need to be ashamed, and which demands to be taken seriously again within the church, in the first place. Therefore, let us consider what practical consequences for the life of the church may result from the biblical doctrine of regeneration.

3
Consequences for the Practice of the Local Church

The testimony to regeneration is as good as silenced in mainline churches. How can we make it heard again? To this question let us formulate a few answers.

First, the seriousness of fallen human nature's complete captivity to death must be seen and pronounced clearly again. Obviously this does not have to be done in every sermon, but wherever the biblical text suggests it, it must be made clear and adequately presented. A clergyman very often meets much good will, much kindness, friendliness and helpfulness in his congregation. We need to be, and should be, thankful for this. But whenever we find ourselves for this reason forgetting that even the nicest person without the new birth cannot see the kingdom of God, then our effective service for God is decisively halted.

Second, we must remember that the new birth cannot be brought about by us. But wherever the gospel of Jesus is clearly proclaimed, there the miracle can be confidently expected. This double recognition frees us from any false optimism, as it also frees us from resignation, when the response to our message is not large. At the same time it gives us joy in our work and in the "success" we meet in small things and in hidden dimensions.

Third, as far as the counseling and the edification of the congregation are concerned, the fact that there are regenerate people (not merely those who have more or less religious interest) demands that we ourselves shall seriously walk God's way with them, thankfully and undismayed by any possible reproach of Pharisaism or preferential treatment. Nor should we be ashamed of those children of God who at times may appear rather peculiar, for God himself is not ashamed of them.

Within the congregation, the particular way of God in the regeneration of individuals is paralleled by care for these individuals. Special priority must be given to their protection and their growth in the faith, their gathering together and above all their being sent out.

A pastoral work, however generously planned and organized, is doomed to fall to spiritual ruin wherever it transgresses these lines which God has set and wishes to reach everybody en masse, starting off on universalist presuppositions.

Fellow workers for the spiritual upbuilding of the church cannot be organized but at most can only be discovered. Those who are born again are born, each in his or her own way, to the task of cultivating and nourishing the life of the church.

Notes

[1]P. J. Spener, *Von der Wiedergeburt*, ed., H. G. Feller (Stuttgart: J. F. Steinkopf, 1963), p. 13.

[2]*Auftrag und Dienst der Volksmission* (Stuttgart: 1967).

[3]Ibid., pp. 26-38.

[4]P. Hefner in *Evangelische Theologie*, 32 (1972), 361.

[5]Jürgen Moltmann in *Evangelische Theologie*, 32 (1972), 315, with a quotation from Jungk & Mundt, *Das Umstrittene Experiment DER MENSCH* (1966).

[6]Experts are without exception very skeptical. According to Moltmann, ex. cit., the thesis of the biological production of a new man "is not expressed by the geneticists without some irony, nor taken seriously by the public without a certain foolishness."

[7]Martin Luther, "Lectures on Galatians, 1535, Chapters 1-4," in *Luther's Works*, by Martin Luther, ed. Jaroslav Pelican (St. Louis: Concordia Publishing House, 1963), XXVI, p. 392.

[8]Ibid., p. 90.

[9]Martin Luther, "A Treatise on Baptism," in *Works of Martin Luther*, trans. C. M. Jacobs (Philadelphia: Muhlenberg Press, 1943), I, 57.

[10]Cf. Thomas Aquinas, *Summa Theologica* (London: Eyre and Spottiswode; New York: McGraw-Hill, 1975), LVII: "But baptism is a spiritual birth" (p. 115); or "Spiritual rebirth which takes place through baptism" (p. 109).

[11]Luther, *Works of Martin Luther*, I, 57.

[12]Ibid. "The sacrament, or sign, of baptism is quickly over, as we plainly see. But the thing it signifies, viz., the spiritual baptism, the drowning of sin, lasts so long as we live . . . . Therefore this whole life is nothing else than a spiritual baptism which does not cease till death." See also Martin Luther, *Luther's Primary Works*, ed. H. Wace and C. A. Buchheim (London: John Murrat, 1883), p. 7, where he discusses the meaning of conversion in the first and best known of the ninety-five theses, "Our Lord and Master Jesus Christ in saying, 'Repent ye,' etc., intended that the whole life of believers should be penitence."

[13]Ibid., I, 58. "So, then, the life of a Christian, from baptism to the grave, is nothing else than the beginning of a blessed death, for at the Last Day God will make him altogether new."

[14]Cf. the later Lutheran confession, the Formula of Concord of 1577, in which the medieval teaching is rejected "that God in the regeneration of man utterly abolishes the substance and essence of the old Adam, and especially the rational soul, and creates from nothing in that conversion and regeneration a new essence of the soul" in Philip Schaff, *The Creeds of Christendom* (New York: Harper and Brothers, 1919), III, 111.

[15]Cf. C. H. Ratschow, *Die eine christliche Taufe* (Gütersloh: Gütersloher Verlagshaus Gerd Mohn, 1972), p. 69.

[16]Cf. H. Diels, *Die Fragmente der Vorsokratiker* (Hamburg, 1972), p. 21ff., especially fragments 12 and 91. In these connections we may also find the reasons for the fact that R. Bultmann could link his existential interpretation of Christian living to the Reformation.

[17]Cf. in the Lutheran confessions: Apologie IV, 78; IV, 125; IV, 292; note especially XII, 1.58 where regeneration is mentioned within the doctrine of repentance, and

expressly of an event *after* baptism; and further in FC Ep. VI, 3; FC SD III, 25; III, 22; etc.

[18]FC SD III, 18ff.

[19]E.g. in FC Ep. VI, 6.

[20]In the process of transmission of teaching by means of the baptismal liturgy the words accompanying the laying on of hands on the baptismal candidate may well have played a special part, and should not be underestimated: "The Almighty God and Father of Our Lord Jesus Christ, who has begotten you anew through water and the Holy Spirit," and in the subsequent prayer of thanks the expression, "We give thee hearty praise and thanks, that thou . . . hast also caused this child to be born again by holy baptism." (Agende für Evang.-Luth. Gemeinden. Hrsg. v.d. Vereinigten Evang.-Luth. Kirche Deutschlands, B. III: Studienausgabe [Berlin: Lutherisches Verlagshaus, 1963], 65).

[21]Albrecht Ritschl, "Instruction in the Christian Religion," trans. Alice Mead Swing, in Albert Temple, *The Theology of Albrecht Ritschl* (London: Longmans, Green & Co., 1901), p. 228.

[22]Ibid.

[23]Karl Barth, *Credo* (New York: Charles Scribner's Sons, 1962), p. 201.

[24]Ibid., p. 202.

[25]O. Weber, *Grundlagen der Dogmatik* (Neukirchen: Verlag der Buchhandlung des Erziehungsvereins, 1962), II, 401.

[26]Ibid.

[27]Ibid., pp. 284f.

[28]Moltmann, *Theology of Hope*, trans. James W. Leitch (New York: Harper & Row, 1965), p. 328.

[29]Ibid., p. 329.

[30]Cf. 2 Peter 3:13. In relying upon a passage such as Matthew 19:28 Moltmann's theological scheme has a certain, though one-sided, justification. In a similar saying of Jesus, Luke reports the words "in my kingdom" (Lk. 22:30) instead of these words.

[31]Cf. F. Büchsel, "ginomai," ThW, I, p. 685ff.

[32]Cf. on this distinction note 38 on John 3. Purely linguistically, both translations are possible.

[33]G. Holtz, "Die Pastoralbriefe," ThHkzNT 13, p. 233 on Titus 3:4.

[34]On Paul cf. A. Oepke, *Der Brief des Paulus an die Galater*, ThHkzNT 9, 2nd ed., p. 89 on Galatians 3:7: "Normally in the case of the baptized, faith and obedience are presupposed—baptism is still missionary and conversion baptism."

[35]The tense used is the aorist participle.

[36]The formulation "the kindness . . . of *God*, . . . in the *Holy Spirit* . . . through *Jesus Christ*" (3:4-6) is remarkable.

[37]The Greek word *anothen* means spatially "from above" and temporally "anew" or "again."

[38]For *gennethenai* the translation "be born" has become usual. In the light of the Semitic background to the tradition of the Gospel of John, it ought really to be translated "to be begotten," as an expression used to denote the male, as distinct from the female, function. The latter was more to the fore in Hellenistic piety. This does not express in the same way as the Semitic tradition's preferred expression *to be begotten*, the radical beginning accomplished by God alone beyond all

our human possibilities. Cf. O. Michel, "Jesus der Jude," in *Der historische Jesus und der kerygmatische Christus,* ed. Ristow and Matthiae (3rd ed., Berlin: Eu: Verlagsanstalt, 1964), p. 313, n. 6.

[39]Cf. J. Schniewind, *Das biblische Wort von der Bekehrung* (Göttingen: Vandenhoeck & Ruprecht, 1948), p. 8. "Baptism means death" with a reference to Mark 10:38 and Luke 12:50.

[40]J. Schniewind, "Von der Neugeburt—Das Gespräch Jesu mit Nikodemus" in *Zur Erneuerung des Christenstandes* (Göttingen: Vandenhoeck & Ruprecht, 1966), p. 30.

[41]However, compare later mention in 7:50 and 19:39.

[42]Cf. e.g., C. K. Barrett, *The Gospel According to St. John* (London: SPCK, 1958), p. 172: "The notion of a supernatural begetting . . . is not found in Paul."

[43]*gennetheis kata pneuma;* cf. *epaggelias tekna* "children of promise" (v. 28).

[44]A. Oepke, op. cit., p. 97, of O. Michel, *Der Brief an die Römer,* 12th ed. (Göttingen: Vandenhoeck & Ruprecht, 1963), p. 197 (on Rom. 8:15).

[45]Cf. also O. Rodenberg, "Heiliger Geist—ein undeutliches Wort?" in *Theologische Beiträge,* II (1971), 169.

[46]Ibid.

[47]The relationship between regeneration and conversion should be dealt with separately. We can only indicate here that by the emphasis on the unilateral activity of God in reference to regeneration, the justification and the necessity of the imperatives in conversion (Mt. 3:2; 4:17) are in no way called into question.

[48]Thus, especially in the Lutheran tradition; cf. FC SD III, 19: *justificatio est regeneratio.*

[49]Thus, especially in the Reformed tradition, cf. John Calvin, *Institutes of the Christian Religion,* III, 11, 1, ed. John T. McNeill, trans. Ford Lewis Battles (Philadelphia: Westminster Press, 1975). "We principally receive a double grace: namely, . . . being reconciled to God through Christ's blamelessness . . . and secondly . . . sanctified by Christ's Spirit . . . of regeneration, indeed, the second of these gifts."

[50]Today this might perhaps be better formulated: so committed, that anger is aroused in them and in their audience over the revolutionaries of "the left" or the exploiters of "the right."

[51]O. Hallesby, *Why I Am a Christian,* trans. Clarence J. Carlsen (Minneapolis: Augsburg Publishing House, 1930), pp. 88-89.

[52]Cf. also 1 Peter 1:23 for the contrast between perishable seed and the abiding, life-creating seed of the Word.

[53]Cf. J. T. Beck, *Die christliche Lehrwissenschaft nach den biblischen Urkunden,* I, 2nd ed. (Stuttgart: J. F. Steinkopf, 1875), p. 535: "Just as God in the Mediator has become his God and Father, so man has become in Him a 'man of God' (2 Tim. 3:17), admittedly only in an initial fashion as a child of God, but nevertheless as certainly and as truly a man of God as a child is a man."

[54]Cf. H. J. Kraus, "Psalmen I" in *Biblischer Kommentar Altes Testament,* XV, 1, 3rd ed. (Neukirchen: Verlag der Buchhandlung des Erziehungsvereins, 1966), p. 389: "Only God's free creative deed can renew the inner being of man. That is the realisation which stands out starkly in the Old Testament and is expressed in the prayers of Psalm 51 . . . . The one who prays . . . appeals in his requests to the great prophetic promises, which in Jeremiah and Ezekiel extend beyond the Old Covenant."

⁵⁵Cf. H. W. Wolff, "The individual and the community," in *Anthropologie des Alten Testaments* (Munich: Chr. Kaiser, 1973), especially p. 320.

⁵⁶Gerhard von Rad, *Old Testament Theology,* trans. D. M. G. Stalker (London: SCM Press, 1965), I, 54ff.

⁵⁷Cf., e.g., on the book of Job, Gerhard von Rad, *Wisdom in Israel,* trans. James D. Martin (London: SCM Press, 1972), p. 207: "We are certainly correct in speaking of a certain gaining of independence on the part of the individual within the cultic community."

⁵⁸Cf. Martin Noth, *The History of Israel,* revised trans. P. R. Ackroyd (London: Adam and Charles Black, 1960), pp. 346ff., 420-21.

⁵⁹As in Friedrich Schleiermacher, *The Christian Faith,* ed. H. R. MacKintosh and J. S. Stewart (Edinburgh: T. & T. Clark, 1928), p. 532: "The Christian church takes shape through the coming together of regenerate individuals to form a system of mutual interaction and cooperation."

⁶⁰Cf. O. Michel, *Das Zeugnis des Neuen Testaments von der Gemeinde* (Göttingen: Vandenhoeck & Ruprecht, 1941), p. 27ff. Against Schleiermacher's sociological understanding of the church, the basic "eschatological-apocalyptic character of the people of God" is stressed here, finding its constitution "through cross, Easter, Ascension and Pentecost" (p. 30).

⁶¹E.g., in 1 Peter 2:9f.; cf. H. Strathmann, *"laos,"* ThW, IV, p. 53ff.

⁶²Deuteronomy 7:7f. and frequently elsewhere.

⁶³That is, the missionary testimony of the Christian can and should be accompanied by social and political involvement as a sign, not only in direct connection with mission, but as the inner consequence of regeneration. The missionary testimony can never in principle be relieved or replaced by this activity.

⁶⁴Cf. Ritschl, "Instruction in the Christian Religion," (p. 227) where he calls regeneration the "ideal beginning of the Christian life."

⁶⁵Cf., on the contrary, J. T. Beck, op. cit., para. 28, p. 536: "The justification which love provides, once it is taken to be a divine declaration mediated by the Word and the calling of the Christian, is, like all other divine speech, an act of declaration with real effective power to change its object."

⁶⁶In contrast to O. Weber, see A. Schlatter, *Das christliche Dogma* (Stuttgart: Verlag der Vereinsbuchhandlung, 1911), p. 505: "Regeneration is not merely a hope, but an event which fashions our history."

⁶⁷See in note 47 the observation that a man can be challenged to be converted but not to be born again. (Jn. 3:3 is mere verification.)

⁶⁸Cf. Colossians 3:3; and Rodenberg, op. cit., p. 170, who speaks in the context of John 3:8 of the "hiddenness of the regenerate."

⁶⁹One biblical narrative gives a classic description of this fact which goes well beyond all abstractions—the account of the dialog between Jesus and Peter in John 21:15ff. The love for Jesus which Peter confesses in response to a threefold question is no deed or virtue on which Peter could or would pride himself in any way, but rather an obligation to Jesus retained through failure (18:27; 21:23) and questioning.

⁷⁰Cf. M. Kähler, *Die Wissenschaft der christlichen Lehre* (rpt. Neukirchen: Verlag der Buchhandlung des Erziehungsvereins, 1966), para. 620 on "Signs by which the presence of new life can rightly be deduced": "For the question in hand the relationship with God is always a prior issue; its correct resolution finds its

expression in the prayer life of the child of God. This event anticipates in a certain sense the fulfillment of the goal which is proper to man. By entering into the offered relationship of communion with God, the sinner accomplishes the decisive step through which he realises his original potential in its most important aspect, and in that communion with the Origin of all personhood gains the *independence* of a personal life in every aspect" (italics not in original).